LIFE COACHING FORMS

INFORMATION			
NAME			
ADDRESS			
EMAIL			
WEBSITE			
PHONE			
EMERGENCY		FAX	
CONTCT PERSON		PHONE	

LOGBOOK INFORMATION			
CONTINUED FROM LOG BOOK		CONTINUED TO LOG BOOK	
LOG START DATE		LOG BOOK END DATE	

NOTES

COACHING LOG

DATE:	VENUE:

CLIENT'S NAME:	

ADDRESS:	

EMAIL:	PHONE NO:
TIME:	DORATION:

TOPIC:

ACTIONS POINTS SINCE THE LAST COACHING SESSION

A.	
B.	
C.	

DISCUSSION SUMMARY

ACTIONS TO WORK ON BEFORE NEXT SESSION

A.	
B.	
C.	

LIGHT BULB MOMENTS

A.	
B.	
C.	

NEXT SESSION DETAILS

NEXT SESSION DATE:	VENUE:
TIME:	DURATION:

NOTES:

COACHING LOG

DATE:	VENUE:

CLIENT'S NAME:	

ADDRESS:	

EMAIL:	PHONE NO:
TIME:	DORATION:

TOPIC:	

ACTIONS POINTS SINCE THE LAST COACHING SESSION

A.	
B.	
C.	

DISCUSSION SUMMARY

ACTIONS TO WORK ON BEFORE NEXT SESSION

A.	
B.	
C.	

LIGHT BULB MOMENTS

A.	
B.	
C.	

NEXT SESSION DETAILS

NEXT SESSION DATE:	VENUE:
TIME:	DURATION:

NOTES:	

COACHING LOG

DATE:	VENUE:

CLIENT'S NAME:

ADDRESS:

EMAIL:	PHONE NO:
TIME:	DORATION:

TOPIC:

ACTIONS POINTS SINCE THE LAST COACHING SESSION

A.	
B.	
C.	

DISCUSSION SUMMARY

ACTIONS TO WORK ON BEFORE NEXT SESSION

A.	
B.	
C.	

LIGHT BULB MOMENTS

A.	
B.	
C.	

NEXT SESSION DETAILS

NEXT SESSION DATE:	VENUE:
TIME:	DURATION:

NOTES:

COACHING LOG

DATE:	VENUE:

CLIENT'S NAME:

ADDRESS:

EMAIL:	PHONE NO:

TIME:	DORATION:

TOPIC:

ACTIONS POINTS SINCE THE LAST COACHING SESSION

A.	
B.	
C.	

DISCUSSION SUMMARY

ACTIONS TO WORK ON BEFORE NEXT SESSION

A.	
B.	
C.	

LIGHT BULB MOMENTS

A.	
B.	
C.	

NEXT SESSION DETAILS

NEXT SESSION DATE:	VENUE:
TIME:	DURATION:

NOTES:

COACHING LOG

DATE:	VENUE:

CLIENT'S NAME:	

ADDRESS:	

EMAIL:	PHONE NO:
TIME:	DORATION:

TOPIC:

ACTIONS POINTS SINCE THE LAST COACHING SESSION

A.	
B.	
C.	

DISCUSSION SUMMARY

ACTIONS TO WORK ON BEFORE NEXT SESSION

A.	
B.	
C.	

LIGHT BULB MOMENTS

A.	
B.	
C.	

NEXT SESSION DETAILS

NEXT SESSION DATE:	VENUE:
TIME:	DURATION:

NOTES:

COACHING LOG

DATE:	VENUE:

| CLIENT'S NAME: | |

| ADDRESS: | |

EMAIL:	PHONE NO:
TIME:	DORATION:

| TOPIC: | |

ACTIONS POINTS SINCE THE LAST COACHING SESSION

A.	
B.	
C.	

DISCUSSION SUMMARY

ACTIONS TO WORK ON BEFORE NEXT SESSION

A.	
B.	
C.	

LIGHT BULB MOMENTS

A.	
B.	
C.	

NEXT SESSION DETAILS

NEXT SESSION DATE:	VENUE:
TIME:	DURATION:

| NOTES: | |

COACHING LOG

DATE:	VENUE:

CLIENT'S NAME:	

ADDRESS:

EMAIL:	PHONE NO:
TIME:	DORATION:

TOPIC:

ACTIONS POINTS SINCE THE LAST COACHING SESSION

A.	
B.	
C.	

DISCUSSION SUMMARY

ACTIONS TO WORK ON BEFORE NEXT SESSION

A.	
B.	
C.	

LIGHT BULB MOMENTS

A.	
B.	
C.	

NEXT SESSION DETAILS

NEXT SESSION DATE:	VENUE:
TIME:	DURATION:

NOTES:

COACHING LOG

DATE:	VENUE:

CLIENT'S NAME:

ADDRESS:

EMAIL:	PHONE NO:
TIME:	DORATION:

TOPIC:

ACTIONS POINTS SINCE THE LAST COACHING SESSION

A.

B.

C.

DISCUSSION SUMMARY

ACTIONS TO WORK ON BEFORE NEXT SESSION

A.

B.

C.

LIGHT BULB MOMENTS

A.

B.

C.

NEXT SESSION DETAILS

NEXT SESSION DATE:	VENUE:
TIME:	DURATION:

NOTES:

COACHING LOG

DATE:	VENUE:

CLIENT'S NAME:	

ADDRESS:	

EMAIL:	PHONE NO:
TIME:	DORATION:

TOPIC:	

ACTIONS POINTS SINCE THE LAST COACHING SESSION

A.

B.

C.

DISCUSSION SUMMARY

ACTIONS TO WORK ON BEFORE NEXT SESSION

A.

B.

C.

LIGHT BULB MOMENTS

A.

B.

C.

NEXT SESSION DETAILS

NEXT SESSION DATE:	VENUE:
TIME:	DURATION:

NOTES:

COACHING LOG

DATE:	VENUE:

CLIENT'S NAME:

ADDRESS:

EMAIL:	PHONE NO:
TIME:	DORATION:

TOPIC:

ACTIONS POINTS SINCE THE LAST COACHING SESSION

A.

B.

C.

DISCUSSION SUMMARY

ACTIONS TO WORK ON BEFORE NEXT SESSION

A.

B.

C.

LIGHT BULB MOMENTS

A.

B.

C.

NEXT SESSION DETAILS

NEXT SESSION DATE:	VENUE:
TIME:	DURATION:

NOTES:

COACHING LOG

DATE:	VENUE:

CLIENT'S NAME:

ADDRESS:

EMAIL:	PHONE NO:
TIME:	DORATION:

TOPIC:

ACTIONS POINTS SINCE THE LAST COACHING SESSION

A.	
B.	
C.	

DISCUSSION SUMMARY

ACTIONS TO WORK ON BEFORE NEXT SESSION

A.	
B.	
C.	

LIGHT BULB MOMENTS

A.	
B.	
C.	

NEXT SESSION DETAILS

NEXT SESSION DATE:	VENUE:
TIME:	DURATION:

NOTES:

COACHING LOG

DATE:	VENUE:

CLIENT'S NAME:

ADDRESS:

EMAIL:	PHONE NO:
TIME:	DORATION:

TOPIC:

ACTIONS POINTS SINCE THE LAST COACHING SESSION

A.	
B.	
C.	

DISCUSSION SUMMARY

ACTIONS TO WORK ON BEFORE NEXT SESSION

A.	
B.	
C.	

LIGHT BULB MOMENTS

A.	
B.	
C.	

NEXT SESSION DETAILS

NEXT SESSION DATE:	VENUE:
TIME:	DURATION:

NOTES:

COACHING LOG

DATE:	VENUE:

CLIENT'S NAME:

ADDRESS:

EMAIL:	PHONE NO:

TIME:	DORATION:

TOPIC:

ACTIONS POINTS SINCE THE LAST COACHING SESSION

A.	
B.	
C.	

DISCUSSION SUMMARY

ACTIONS TO WORK ON BEFORE NEXT SESSION

A.	
B.	
C.	

LIGHT BULB MOMENTS

A.	
B.	
C.	

NEXT SESSION DETAILS

NEXT SESSION DATE:	VENUE:
TIME:	DURATION:

NOTES:

COACHING LOG

DATE:	VENUE:

CLIENT'S NAME:

ADDRESS:

EMAIL:	PHONE NO:
TIME:	DORATION:

TOPIC:

ACTIONS POINTS SINCE THE LAST COACHING SESSION

A.	
B.	
C.	

DISCUSSION SUMMARY

ACTIONS TO WORK ON BEFORE NEXT SESSION

A.	
B.	
C.	

LIGHT BULB MOMENTS

A.	
B.	
C.	

NEXT SESSION DETAILS

NEXT SESSION DATE:	VENUE:
TIME:	DURATION:

NOTES:

COACHING LOG

DATE:	VENUE:

CLIENT'S NAME:

ADDRESS:

EMAIL:	PHONE NO:
TIME:	DORATION:

TOPIC:

ACTIONS POINTS SINCE THE LAST COACHING SESSION

A.

B.

C.

DISCUSSION SUMMARY

ACTIONS TO WORK ON BEFORE NEXT SESSION

A.

B.

C.

LIGHT BULB MOMENTS

A.

B.

C.

NEXT SESSION DETAILS

NEXT SESSION DATE:	VENUE:
TIME:	DURATION:

NOTES:

COACHING LOG

DATE:	VENUE:

| CLIENT'S NAME: | |

| ADDRESS: | |
| | |

| EMAIL: | PHONE NO: |
| TIME: | DORATION: |

TOPIC:

ACTIONS POINTS SINCE THE LAST COACHING SESSION

A.	
B.	
C.	

DISCUSSION SUMMARY

ACTIONS TO WORK ON BEFORE NEXT SESSION

A.	
B.	
C.	

LIGHT BULB MOMENTS

A.	
B.	
C.	

NEXT SESSION DETAILS

NEXT SESSION DATE:	VENUE:
TIME:	DURATION:

NOTES:

COACHING LOG

DATE:	VENUE:

CLIENT'S NAME:

ADDRESS:

EMAIL:	PHONE NO:
TIME:	DORATION:

TOPIC:

ACTIONS POINTS SINCE THE LAST COACHING SESSION

A.	
B.	
C.	

DISCUSSION SUMMARY

ACTIONS TO WORK ON BEFORE NEXT SESSION

A.	
B.	
C.	

LIGHT BULB MOMENTS

A.	
B.	
C.	

NEXT SESSION DETAILS

NEXT SESSION DATE:	VENUE:
TIME:	DURATION:

NOTES:

COACHING LOG

DATE:	VENUE:

CLIENT'S NAME:

ADDRESS:

EMAIL:	PHONE NO:
TIME:	DORATION:

TOPIC:

ACTIONS POINTS SINCE THE LAST COACHING SESSION

A.

B.

C.

DISCUSSION SUMMARY

ACTIONS TO WORK ON BEFORE NEXT SESSION

A.

B.

C.

LIGHT BULB MOMENTS

A.

B.

C.

NEXT SESSION DETAILS

NEXT SESSION DATE:	VENUE:
TIME:	DURATION:

NOTES:

COACHING LOG

DATE:	VENUE:

CLIENT'S NAME:

ADDRESS:

EMAIL:	PHONE NO:
TIME:	DORATION:

TOPIC:

ACTIONS POINTS SINCE THE LAST COACHING SESSION

A.	
B.	
C.	

DISCUSSION SUMMARY

ACTIONS TO WORK ON BEFORE NEXT SESSION

A.	
B.	
C.	

LIGHT BULB MOMENTS

A.	
B.	
C.	

NEXT SESSION DETAILS

NEXT SESSION DATE:	VENUE:
TIME:	DURATION:

NOTES:

COACHING LOG

DATE:	VENUE:

CLIENT'S NAME:

ADDRESS:

EMAIL:	PHONE NO:
TIME:	DORATION:

TOPIC:

ACTIONS POINTS SINCE THE LAST COACHING SESSION

A.	
B.	
C.	

DISCUSSION SUMMARY

ACTIONS TO WORK ON BEFORE NEXT SESSION

A.	
B.	
C.	

LIGHT BULB MOMENTS

A.	
B.	
C.	

NEXT SESSION DETAILS

NEXT SESSION DATE:	VENUE:
TIME:	DURATION:

NOTES:

COACHING LOG

DATE:	VENUE:

CLIENT'S NAME:

ADDRESS:

EMAIL:	PHONE NO:
TIME:	DORATION:

TOPIC:

ACTIONS POINTS SINCE THE LAST COACHING SESSION

A.	
B.	
C.	

DISCUSSION SUMMARY

ACTIONS TO WORK ON BEFORE NEXT SESSION

A.	
B.	
C.	

LIGHT BULB MOMENTS

A.	
B.	
C.	

NEXT SESSION DETAILS

NEXT SESSION DATE:	VENUE:
TIME:	DURATION:

NOTES:

COACHING LOG

DATE:	VENUE:

CLIENT'S NAME:

ADDRESS:

EMAIL:	PHONE NO:
TIME:	DORATION:

TOPIC:

ACTIONS POINTS SINCE THE LAST COACHING SESSION

A.	
B.	
C.	

DISCUSSION SUMMARY

ACTIONS TO WORK ON BEFORE NEXT SESSION

A.	
B.	
C.	

LIGHT BULB MOMENTS

A.	
B.	
C.	

NEXT SESSION DETAILS

NEXT SESSION DATE:	VENUE:
TIME:	DURATION:

NOTES:

COACHING LOG

DATE:	VENUE:

CLIENT'S NAME:	

ADDRESS:	

EMAIL:	PHONE NO:
TIME:	DORATION:

TOPIC:	

ACTIONS POINTS SINCE THE LAST COACHING SESSION

A.	
B.	
C.	

DISCUSSION SUMMARY

ACTIONS TO WORK ON BEFORE NEXT SESSION

A.	
B.	
C.	

LIGHT BULB MOMENTS

A.	
B.	
C.	

NEXT SESSION DETAILS

NEXT SESSION DATE:	VENUE:
TIME:	DURATION:

NOTES:	

COACHING LOG

DATE:	VENUE:

CLIENT'S NAME:

ADDRESS:

EMAIL:	PHONE NO:
TIME:	DORATION:

TOPIC:

ACTIONS POINTS SINCE THE LAST COACHING SESSION

A.	
B.	
C.	

DISCUSSION SUMMARY

ACTIONS TO WORK ON BEFORE NEXT SESSION

A.	
B.	
C.	

LIGHT BULB MOMENTS

A.	
B.	
C.	

NEXT SESSION DETAILS

NEXT SESSION DATE:	VENUE:
TIME:	DURATION:

NOTES:

COACHING LOG

DATE:	VENUE:

CLIENT'S NAME:

ADDRESS:

EMAIL:	PHONE NO:
TIME:	DORATION:

TOPIC:

ACTIONS POINTS SINCE THE LAST COACHING SESSION

A.	
B.	
C.	

DISCUSSION SUMMARY

ACTIONS TO WORK ON BEFORE NEXT SESSION

A.	
B.	
C.	

LIGHT BULB MOMENTS

A.	
B.	
C.	

NEXT SESSION DETAILS

NEXT SESSION DATE:	VENUE:
TIME:	DURATION:

NOTES:

COACHING LOG

DATE:	VENUE:

CLIENT'S NAME:

ADDRESS:

EMAIL:	PHONE NO:
TIME:	DORATION:

TOPIC:

ACTIONS POINTS SINCE THE LAST COACHING SESSION

A.	
B.	
C.	

DISCUSSION SUMMARY

ACTIONS TO WORK ON BEFORE NEXT SESSION

A.	
B.	
C.	

LIGHT BULB MOMENTS

A.	
B.	
C.	

NEXT SESSION DETAILS

NEXT SESSION DATE:	VENUE:
TIME:	DURATION:

NOTES:

COACHING LOG

DATE:	VENUE:

CLIENT'S NAME:

ADDRESS:

EMAIL:	PHONE NO:
TIME:	DORATION:

TOPIC:

ACTIONS POINTS SINCE THE LAST COACHING SESSION

A.	
B.	
C.	

DISCUSSION SUMMARY

ACTIONS TO WORK ON BEFORE NEXT SESSION

A.	
B.	
C.	

LIGHT BULB MOMENTS

A.	
B.	
C.	

NEXT SESSION DETAILS

NEXT SESSION DATE:	VENUE:
TIME:	DURATION:

NOTES:

COACHING LOG

DATE:	VENUE:

CLIENT'S NAME:

ADDRESS:

EMAIL:	PHONE NO:
TIME:	DORATION:

TOPIC:

ACTIONS POINTS SINCE THE LAST COACHING SESSION

A.	
B.	
C.	

DISCUSSION SUMMARY

ACTIONS TO WORK ON BEFORE NEXT SESSION

A.	
B.	
C.	

LIGHT BULB MOMENTS

A.	
B.	
C.	

NEXT SESSION DETAILS

NEXT SESSION DATE:	VENUE:
TIME:	DURATION:

NOTES:

COACHING LOG

DATE:	VENUE:

CLIENT'S NAME:

ADDRESS:

EMAIL:	PHONE NO:
TIME:	DORATION:

TOPIC:

ACTIONS POINTS SINCE THE LAST COACHING SESSION

A.

B.

C.

DISCUSSION SUMMARY

ACTIONS TO WORK ON BEFORE NEXT SESSION

A.

B.

C.

LIGHT BULB MOMENTS

A.

B.

C.

NEXT SESSION DETAILS

NEXT SESSION DATE:	VENUE:
TIME:	DURATION:

NOTES:

COACHING LOG

DATE:	VENUE:

CLIENT'S NAME:

ADDRESS:

EMAIL:	PHONE NO:
TIME:	DORATION:

TOPIC:

ACTIONS POINTS SINCE THE LAST COACHING SESSION

A.

B.

C.

DISCUSSION SUMMARY

ACTIONS TO WORK ON BEFORE NEXT SESSION

A.

B.

C.

LIGHT BULB MOMENTS

A.

B.

C.

NEXT SESSION DETAILS

NEXT SESSION DATE:	VENUE:
TIME:	DURATION:

NOTES:

COACHING LOG

DATE:	VENUE:

CLIENT'S NAME:	

ADDRESS:	

EMAIL:	PHONE NO:
TIME:	DORATION:

TOPIC:

ACTIONS POINTS SINCE THE LAST COACHING SESSION

A.	
B.	
C.	

DISCUSSION SUMMARY

ACTIONS TO WORK ON BEFORE NEXT SESSION

A.	
B.	
C.	

LIGHT BULB MOMENTS

A.	
B.	
C.	

NEXT SESSION DETAILS

NEXT SESSION DATE:	VENUE:
TIME:	DURATION:

NOTES:

COACHING LOG

DATE:	VENUE:

CLIENT'S NAME:	

ADDRESS:	

EMAIL:	PHONE NO:
TIME:	DORATION:

TOPIC:	

ACTIONS POINTS SINCE THE LAST COACHING SESSION

A.	
B.	
C.	

DISCUSSION SUMMARY

ACTIONS TO WORK ON BEFORE NEXT SESSION

A.	
B.	
C.	

LIGHT BULB MOMENTS

A.	
B.	
C.	

NEXT SESSION DETAILS

NEXT SESSION DATE:	VENUE:
TIME:	DURATION:

NOTES:	

COACHING LOG

DATE:	VENUE:

CLIENT'S NAME:

ADDRESS:

EMAIL:	PHONE NO:
TIME:	DORATION:

TOPIC:

ACTIONS POINTS SINCE THE LAST COACHING SESSION

A.	
B.	
C.	

DISCUSSION SUMMARY

ACTIONS TO WORK ON BEFORE NEXT SESSION

A.	
B.	
C.	

LIGHT BULB MOMENTS

A.	
B.	
C.	

NEXT SESSION DETAILS

NEXT SESSION DATE:	VENUE:
TIME:	DURATION:

NOTES:

COACHING LOG

DATE:	VENUE:

CLIENT'S NAME:	

ADDRESS:	

EMAIL:	PHONE NO:
TIME:	DORATION:

TOPIC:	

ACTIONS POINTS SINCE THE LAST COACHING SESSION

A.	
B.	
C.	

DISCUSSION SUMMARY

ACTIONS TO WORK ON BEFORE NEXT SESSION

A.	
B.	
C.	

LIGHT BULB MOMENTS

A.	
B.	
C.	

NEXT SESSION DETAILS

NEXT SESSION DATE:	VENUE:
TIME:	DURATION:

NOTES:	

COACHING LOG

DATE:	VENUE:

CLIENT'S NAME:	

ADDRESS:	

EMAIL:	PHONE NO:
TIME:	DORATION:

TOPIC:	

ACTIONS POINTS SINCE THE LAST COACHING SESSION

A.	
B.	
C.	

DISCUSSION SUMMARY

ACTIONS TO WORK ON BEFORE NEXT SESSION

A.	
B.	
C.	

LIGHT BULB MOMENTS

A.	
B.	
C.	

NEXT SESSION DETAILS

NEXT SESSION DATE:	VENUE:
TIME:	DURATION:

NOTES:	

COACHING LOG

DATE:	VENUE:

CLIENT'S NAME:

ADDRESS:

EMAIL:	PHONE NO:
TIME:	DORATION:

TOPIC:

ACTIONS POINTS SINCE THE LAST COACHING SESSION

A.	
B.	
C.	

DISCUSSION SUMMARY

ACTIONS TO WORK ON BEFORE NEXT SESSION

A.	
B.	
C.	

LIGHT BULB MOMENTS

A.	
B.	
C.	

NEXT SESSION DETAILS

NEXT SESSION DATE:	VENUE:
TIME:	DURATION:

NOTES:

COACHING LOG

DATE:	VENUE:

CLIENT'S NAME:

ADDRESS:

EMAIL:	PHONE NO:
TIME:	DORATION:

TOPIC:

ACTIONS POINTS SINCE THE LAST COACHING SESSION

A.	
B.	
C.	

DISCUSSION SUMMARY

ACTIONS TO WORK ON BEFORE NEXT SESSION

A.	
B.	
C.	

LIGHT BULB MOMENTS

A.	
B.	
C.	

NEXT SESSION DETAILS

NEXT SESSION DATE:	VENUE:
TIME:	DURATION:

NOTES:

COACHING LOG

DATE:	VENUE:

CLIENT'S NAME:

ADDRESS:

EMAIL:	PHONE NO:
TIME:	DORATION:

TOPIC:

ACTIONS POINTS SINCE THE LAST COACHING SESSION

A.	
B.	
C.	

DISCUSSION SUMMARY

ACTIONS TO WORK ON BEFORE NEXT SESSION

A.	
B.	
C.	

LIGHT BULB MOMENTS

A.	
B.	
C.	

NEXT SESSION DETAILS

NEXT SESSION DATE:	VENUE:
TIME:	DURATION:

NOTES:

COACHING LOG

DATE:	VENUE:

CLIENT'S NAME:
ADDRESS:

EMAIL:	PHONE NO:
TIME:	DORATION:

TOPIC:

ACTIONS POINTS SINCE THE LAST COACHING SESSION

A.	
B.	
C.	

DISCUSSION SUMMARY

ACTIONS TO WORK ON BEFORE NEXT SESSION

A.	
B.	
C.	

LIGHT BULB MOMENTS

A.	
B.	
C.	

NEXT SESSION DETAILS

NEXT SESSION DATE:	VENUE:
TIME:	DURATION:

NOTES:

COACHING LOG

DATE:	VENUE:

CLIENT'S NAME:

ADDRESS:

EMAIL:	PHONE NO:
TIME:	DORATION:

TOPIC:

ACTIONS POINTS SINCE THE LAST COACHING SESSION

A.	
B.	
C.	

DISCUSSION SUMMARY

ACTIONS TO WORK ON BEFORE NEXT SESSION

A.	
B.	
C.	

LIGHT BULB MOMENTS

A.	
B.	
C.	

NEXT SESSION DETAILS

NEXT SESSION DATE:	VENUE:
TIME:	DURATION:

NOTES:

COACHING LOG

DATE:	VENUE:

CLIENT'S NAME:

ADDRESS:

EMAIL:	PHONE NO:

TIME:	DORATION:

TOPIC:

ACTIONS POINTS SINCE THE LAST COACHING SESSION

A.

B.

C.

DISCUSSION SUMMARY

ACTIONS TO WORK ON BEFORE NEXT SESSION

A.

B.

C.

LIGHT BULB MOMENTS

A.

B.

C.

NEXT SESSION DETAILS

NEXT SESSION DATE:	VENUE:

TIME:	DURATION:

NOTES:

COACHING LOG

DATE:	VENUE:

CLIENT'S NAME:

ADDRESS:

EMAIL:	PHONE NO:
TIME:	DORATION:

TOPIC:

ACTIONS POINTS SINCE THE LAST COACHING SESSION

A.	
B.	
C.	

DISCUSSION SUMMARY

ACTIONS TO WORK ON BEFORE NEXT SESSION

A.	
B.	
C.	

LIGHT BULB MOMENTS

A.	
B.	
C.	

NEXT SESSION DETAILS

NEXT SESSION DATE:	VENUE:
TIME:	DURATION:

NOTES:

COACHING LOG

DATE:	VENUE:

CLIENT'S NAME:

ADDRESS:

EMAIL:	PHONE NO:
TIME:	DORATION:

TOPIC:

ACTIONS POINTS SINCE THE LAST COACHING SESSION

A.	
B.	
C.	

DISCUSSION SUMMARY

ACTIONS TO WORK ON BEFORE NEXT SESSION

A.	
B.	
C.	

LIGHT BULB MOMENTS

A.	
B.	
C.	

NEXT SESSION DETAILS

NEXT SESSION DATE:	VENUE:
TIME:	DURATION:

NOTES:

COACHING LOG

DATE:	VENUE:

CLIENT'S NAME:

ADDRESS:

EMAIL:	PHONE NO:
TIME:	DORATION:

TOPIC:

ACTIONS POINTS SINCE THE LAST COACHING SESSION

A.	
B.	
C.	

DISCUSSION SUMMARY

ACTIONS TO WORK ON BEFORE NEXT SESSION

A.	
B.	
C.	

LIGHT BULB MOMENTS

A.	
B.	
C.	

NEXT SESSION DETAILS

NEXT SESSION DATE:	VENUE:
TIME:	DURATION:

NOTES:

COACHING LOG

DATE:	VENUE:

CLIENT'S NAME:

ADDRESS:

EMAIL:	PHONE NO:
TIME:	DORATION:

TOPIC:

ACTIONS POINTS SINCE THE LAST COACHING SESSION

A.	
B.	
C.	

DISCUSSION SUMMARY

ACTIONS TO WORK ON BEFORE NEXT SESSION

A.	
B.	
C.	

LIGHT BULB MOMENTS

A.	
B.	
C.	

NEXT SESSION DETAILS

NEXT SESSION DATE:	VENUE:
TIME:	DURATION:

NOTES:

COACHING LOG

DATE:	VENUE:

CLIENT'S NAME:

ADDRESS:

EMAIL:	PHONE NO:
TIME:	DORATION:

TOPIC:

ACTIONS POINTS SINCE THE LAST COACHING SESSION

A.	
B.	
C.	

DISCUSSION SUMMARY

ACTIONS TO WORK ON BEFORE NEXT SESSION

A.	
B.	
C.	

LIGHT BULB MOMENTS

A.	
B.	
C.	

NEXT SESSION DETAILS

NEXT SESSION DATE:	VENUE:
TIME:	DURATION:

NOTES:

COACHING LOG

DATE:	VENUE:

CLIENT'S NAME:

ADDRESS:

EMAIL:	PHONE NO:
TIME:	DORATION:

TOPIC:

ACTIONS POINTS SINCE THE LAST COACHING SESSION

A.	
B.	
C.	

DISCUSSION SUMMARY

ACTIONS TO WORK ON BEFORE NEXT SESSION

A.	
B.	
C.	

LIGHT BULB MOMENTS

A.	
B.	
C.	

NEXT SESSION DETAILS

NEXT SESSION DATE:	VENUE:
TIME:	DURATION:

NOTES:

COACHING LOG

DATE:	VENUE:

CLIENT'S NAME:

ADDRESS:

EMAIL:	PHONE NO:
TIME:	DORATION:

TOPIC:

ACTIONS POINTS SINCE THE LAST COACHING SESSION

A.	
B.	
C.	

DISCUSSION SUMMARY

ACTIONS TO WORK ON BEFORE NEXT SESSION

A.	
B.	
C.	

LIGHT BULB MOMENTS

A.	
B.	
C.	

NEXT SESSION DETAILS

NEXT SESSION DATE:	VENUE:
TIME:	DURATION:

NOTES:

COACHING LOG

DATE:	VENUE:

CLIENT'S NAME:

ADDRESS:

EMAIL:	PHONE NO:
TIME:	DORATION:

TOPIC:

ACTIONS POINTS SINCE THE LAST COACHING SESSION

A.	
B.	
C.	

DISCUSSION SUMMARY

ACTIONS TO WORK ON BEFORE NEXT SESSION

A.	
B.	
C.	

LIGHT BULB MOMENTS

A.	
B.	
C.	

NEXT SESSION DETAILS

NEXT SESSION DATE:	VENUE:
TIME:	DURATION:

NOTES:

COACHING LOG

DATE:	VENUE:

CLIENT'S NAME:

ADDRESS:

EMAIL:	PHONE NO:

TIME:	DORATION:

TOPIC:

ACTIONS POINTS SINCE THE LAST COACHING SESSION

A.	
B.	
C.	

DISCUSSION SUMMARY

ACTIONS TO WORK ON BEFORE NEXT SESSION

A.	
B.	
C.	

LIGHT BULB MOMENTS

A.	
B.	
C.	

NEXT SESSION DETAILS

NEXT SESSION DATE:	VENUE:
TIME:	DURATION:

NOTES:

COACHING LOG

DATE:	VENUE:

CLIENT'S NAME:

ADDRESS:

EMAIL:	PHONE NO:
TIME:	DORATION:

TOPIC:

ACTIONS POINTS SINCE THE LAST COACHING SESSION

A.	
B.	
C.	

DISCUSSION SUMMARY

ACTIONS TO WORK ON BEFORE NEXT SESSION

A.	
B.	
C.	

LIGHT BULB MOMENTS

A.	
B.	
C.	

NEXT SESSION DETAILS

NEXT SESSION DATE:	VENUE:
TIME:	DURATION:

NOTES:

COACHING LOG

DATE:	VENUE:

CLIENT'S NAME:

ADDRESS:

EMAIL:	PHONE NO:
TIME:	DORATION:

TOPIC:

ACTIONS POINTS SINCE THE LAST COACHING SESSION

A.	
B.	
C.	

DISCUSSION SUMMARY

ACTIONS TO WORK ON BEFORE NEXT SESSION

A.	
B.	
C.	

LIGHT BULB MOMENTS

A.	
B.	
C.	

NEXT SESSION DETAILS

NEXT SESSION DATE:	VENUE:
TIME:	DURATION:

NOTES:

COACHING LOG

DATE:	VENUE:

CLIENT'S NAME:

ADDRESS:

EMAIL:	PHONE NO:
TIME:	DORATION:

TOPIC:

ACTIONS POINTS SINCE THE LAST COACHING SESSION

A.

B.

C.

DISCUSSION SUMMARY

ACTIONS TO WORK ON BEFORE NEXT SESSION

A.

B.

C.

LIGHT BULB MOMENTS

A.

B.

C.

NEXT SESSION DETAILS

NEXT SESSION DATE:	VENUE:
TIME:	DURATION:

NOTES:

COACHING LOG

DATE:	VENUE:

CLIENT'S NAME:

ADDRESS:

EMAIL:	PHONE NO:
TIME:	DORATION:

TOPIC:

ACTIONS POINTS SINCE THE LAST COACHING SESSION

A.	
B.	
C.	

DISCUSSION SUMMARY

ACTIONS TO WORK ON BEFORE NEXT SESSION

A.	
B.	
C.	

LIGHT BULB MOMENTS

A.	
B.	
C.	

NEXT SESSION DETAILS

NEXT SESSION DATE:	VENUE:
TIME:	DURATION:

NOTES:

COACHING LOG

DATE:	VENUE:

CLIENT'S NAME:

ADDRESS:

EMAIL:	PHONE NO:
TIME:	DORATION:

TOPIC:

ACTIONS POINTS SINCE THE LAST COACHING SESSION

A.	
B.	
C.	

DISCUSSION SUMMARY

ACTIONS TO WORK ON BEFORE NEXT SESSION

A.	
B.	
C.	

LIGHT BULB MOMENTS

A.	
B.	
C.	

NEXT SESSION DETAILS

NEXT SESSION DATE:	VENUE:
TIME:	DURATION:

NOTES:

COACHING LOG

DATE:	VENUE:

CLIENT'S NAME:

ADDRESS:

EMAIL:	PHONE NO:
TIME:	DORATION:

TOPIC:

ACTIONS POINTS SINCE THE LAST COACHING SESSION

A.	
B.	
C.	

DISCUSSION SUMMARY

ACTIONS TO WORK ON BEFORE NEXT SESSION

A.	
B.	
C.	

LIGHT BULB MOMENTS

A.	
B.	
C.	

NEXT SESSION DETAILS

NEXT SESSION DATE:	VENUE:
TIME:	DURATION:

NOTES:

COACHING LOG

DATE:	VENUE:

CLIENT'S NAME:

ADDRESS:

EMAIL:	PHONE NO:
TIME:	DORATION:

TOPIC:

ACTIONS POINTS SINCE THE LAST COACHING SESSION

A.	
B.	
C.	

DISCUSSION SUMMARY

ACTIONS TO WORK ON BEFORE NEXT SESSION

A.	
B.	
C.	

LIGHT BULB MOMENTS

A.	
B.	
C.	

NEXT SESSION DETAILS

NEXT SESSION DATE:	VENUE:
TIME:	DURATION:

NOTES:

COACHING LOG

DATE:	VENUE:

CLIENT'S NAME:	

ADDRESS:	

EMAIL:	PHONE NO:
TIME:	DORATION:

TOPIC:

ACTIONS POINTS SINCE THE LAST COACHING SESSION

A.	
B.	
C.	

DISCUSSION SUMMARY

ACTIONS TO WORK ON BEFORE NEXT SESSION

A.	
B.	
C.	

LIGHT BULB MOMENTS

A.	
B.	
C.	

NEXT SESSION DETAILS

NEXT SESSION DATE:	VENUE:
TIME:	DURATION:

NOTES:

COACHING LOG

DATE:	VENUE:

CLIENT'S NAME:

ADDRESS:

EMAIL:	PHONE NO:
TIME:	DORATION:

TOPIC:

ACTIONS POINTS SINCE THE LAST COACHING SESSION

A.	
B.	
C.	

DISCUSSION SUMMARY

ACTIONS TO WORK ON BEFORE NEXT SESSION

A.	
B.	
C.	

LIGHT BULB MOMENTS

A.	
B.	
C.	

NEXT SESSION DETAILS

NEXT SESSION DATE:	VENUE:
TIME:	DURATION:

NOTES:

COACHING LOG

DATE:	VENUE:

CLIENT'S NAME:

ADDRESS:

EMAIL:	PHONE NO:
TIME:	DORATION:

TOPIC:

ACTIONS POINTS SINCE THE LAST COACHING SESSION

A.	
B.	
C.	

DISCUSSION SUMMARY

ACTIONS TO WORK ON BEFORE NEXT SESSION

A.	
B.	
C.	

LIGHT BULB MOMENTS

A.	
B.	
C.	

NEXT SESSION DETAILS

NEXT SESSION DATE:	VENUE:
TIME:	DURATION:

NOTES:

COACHING LOG

DATE:	VENUE:

CLIENT'S NAME:	

ADDRESS:	

EMAIL:	PHONE NO:
TIME:	DORATION:

TOPIC:	

ACTIONS POINTS SINCE THE LAST COACHING SESSION

A.	
B.	
C.	

DISCUSSION SUMMARY

ACTIONS TO WORK ON BEFORE NEXT SESSION

A.	
B.	
C.	

LIGHT BULB MOMENTS

A.	
B.	
C.	

NEXT SESSION DETAILS

NEXT SESSION DATE:	VENUE:
TIME:	DURATION:

NOTES:	

COACHING LOG

DATE:	VENUE:

CLIENT'S NAME:

ADDRESS:

EMAIL:	PHONE NO:
TIME:	DORATION:

TOPIC:

ACTIONS POINTS SINCE THE LAST COACHING SESSION

A.	
B.	
C.	

DISCUSSION SUMMARY

ACTIONS TO WORK ON BEFORE NEXT SESSION

A.	
B.	
C.	

LIGHT BULB MOMENTS

A.	
B.	
C.	

NEXT SESSION DETAILS

NEXT SESSION DATE:	VENUE:
TIME:	DURATION:

NOTES:

COACHING LOG

DATE:	VENUE:

CLIENT'S NAME:

ADDRESS:

EMAIL:	PHONE NO:
TIME:	DORATION:

TOPIC:

ACTIONS POINTS SINCE THE LAST COACHING SESSION

A.

B.

C.

DISCUSSION SUMMARY

ACTIONS TO WORK ON BEFORE NEXT SESSION

A.

B.

C.

LIGHT BULB MOMENTS

A.

B.

C.

NEXT SESSION DETAILS

NEXT SESSION DATE:	VENUE:
TIME:	DURATION:

NOTES:

COACHING LOG

DATE:	VENUE:

CLIENT'S NAME:

ADDRESS:

EMAIL:	PHONE NO:
TIME:	DORATION:

TOPIC:

ACTIONS POINTS SINCE THE LAST COACHING SESSION

A.

B.

C.

DISCUSSION SUMMARY

ACTIONS TO WORK ON BEFORE NEXT SESSION

A.

B.

C.

LIGHT BULB MOMENTS

A.

B.

C.

NEXT SESSION DETAILS

NEXT SESSION DATE:	VENUE:
TIME:	DURATION:

NOTES:

COACHING LOG

DATE:	VENUE:

CLIENT'S NAME:

ADDRESS:

EMAIL:	PHONE NO:
TIME:	DORATION:

TOPIC:

ACTIONS POINTS SINCE THE LAST COACHING SESSION

A.

B.

C.

DISCUSSION SUMMARY

ACTIONS TO WORK ON BEFORE NEXT SESSION

A.

B.

C.

LIGHT BULB MOMENTS

A.

B.

C.

NEXT SESSION DETAILS

NEXT SESSION DATE:	VENUE:
TIME:	DURATION:

NOTES:

COACHING LOG

DATE:	VENUE:

CLIENT'S NAME:	

ADDRESS:	

EMAIL:	PHONE NO:
TIME:	DORATION:

TOPIC:	

ACTIONS POINTS SINCE THE LAST COACHING SESSION

A.	
B.	
C.	

DISCUSSION SUMMARY

ACTIONS TO WORK ON BEFORE NEXT SESSION

A.	
B.	
C.	

LIGHT BULB MOMENTS

A.	
B.	
C.	

NEXT SESSION DETAILS

NEXT SESSION DATE:	VENUE:
TIME:	DURATION:

NOTES:	

COACHING LOG

DATE: | **VENUE:**

CLIENT'S NAME:

ADDRESS:

EMAIL: | **PHONE NO:**

TIME: | **DORATION:**

TOPIC:

ACTIONS POINTS SINCE THE LAST COACHING SESSION

A.

B.

C.

DISCUSSION SUMMARY

ACTIONS TO WORK ON BEFORE NEXT SESSION

A.

B.

C.

LIGHT BULB MOMENTS

A.

B.

C.

NEXT SESSION DETAILS

NEXT SESSION DATE: | **VENUE:**

TIME: | **DURATION:**

NOTES:

COACHING LOG

DATE:	VENUE:

CLIENT'S NAME:

ADDRESS:

EMAIL:	PHONE NO:
TIME:	DORATION:

TOPIC:

ACTIONS POINTS SINCE THE LAST COACHING SESSION

A.	
B.	
C.	

DISCUSSION SUMMARY

ACTIONS TO WORK ON BEFORE NEXT SESSION

A.	
B.	
C.	

LIGHT BULB MOMENTS

A.	
B.	
C.	

NEXT SESSION DETAILS

NEXT SESSION DATE:	VENUE:
TIME:	DURATION:

NOTES:

COACHING LOG

DATE:	VENUE:

CLIENT'S NAME:

ADDRESS:

EMAIL:	PHONE NO:
TIME:	DORATION:

TOPIC:

ACTIONS POINTS SINCE THE LAST COACHING SESSION

A.	
B.	
C.	

DISCUSSION SUMMARY

ACTIONS TO WORK ON BEFORE NEXT SESSION

A.	
B.	
C.	

LIGHT BULB MOMENTS

A.	
B.	
C.	

NEXT SESSION DETAILS

NEXT SESSION DATE:	VENUE:
TIME:	DURATION:

NOTES:

COACHING LOG

DATE:	VENUE:

CLIENT'S NAME:

ADDRESS:

EMAIL:	PHONE NO:

TIME:	DORATION:

TOPIC:

ACTIONS POINTS SINCE THE LAST COACHING SESSION

A.	
B.	
C.	

DISCUSSION SUMMARY

ACTIONS TO WORK ON BEFORE NEXT SESSION

A.	
B.	
C.	

LIGHT BULB MOMENTS

A.	
B.	
C.	

NEXT SESSION DETAILS

NEXT SESSION DATE:	VENUE:
TIME:	DURATION:

NOTES:

COACHING LOG

DATE:	VENUE:

CLIENT'S NAME:

ADDRESS:

EMAIL:	PHONE NO:
TIME:	DORATION:

TOPIC:

ACTIONS POINTS SINCE THE LAST COACHING SESSION

A.

B.

C.

DISCUSSION SUMMARY

ACTIONS TO WORK ON BEFORE NEXT SESSION

A.

B.

C.

LIGHT BULB MOMENTS

A.

B.

C.

NEXT SESSION DETAILS

NEXT SESSION DATE:	VENUE:
TIME:	DURATION:

NOTES:

COACHING LOG

DATE:	VENUE:

CLIENT'S NAME:

ADDRESS:

EMAIL:	PHONE NO:
TIME:	DORATION:

TOPIC:

ACTIONS POINTS SINCE THE LAST COACHING SESSION

A.	
B.	
C.	

DISCUSSION SUMMARY

ACTIONS TO WORK ON BEFORE NEXT SESSION

A.	
B.	
C.	

LIGHT BULB MOMENTS

A.	
B.	
C.	

NEXT SESSION DETAILS

NEXT SESSION DATE:	VENUE:
TIME:	DURATION:

NOTES:

COACHING LOG

DATE:	VENUE:

CLIENT'S NAME:

ADDRESS:

EMAIL:	PHONE NO:
TIME:	DORATION:

TOPIC:

ACTIONS POINTS SINCE THE LAST COACHING SESSION

A.	
B.	
C.	

DISCUSSION SUMMARY

ACTIONS TO WORK ON BEFORE NEXT SESSION

A.	
B.	
C.	

LIGHT BULB MOMENTS

A.	
B.	
C.	

NEXT SESSION DETAILS

NEXT SESSION DATE:	VENUE:
TIME:	DURATION:

NOTES:

COACHING LOG

DATE:	VENUE:

CLIENT'S NAME:	

ADDRESS:	

EMAIL:	PHONE NO:
TIME:	DORATION:

TOPIC:	

ACTIONS POINTS SINCE THE LAST COACHING SESSION

A.	
B.	
C.	

DISCUSSION SUMMARY

ACTIONS TO WORK ON BEFORE NEXT SESSION

A.	
B.	
C.	

LIGHT BULB MOMENTS

A.	
B.	
C.	

NEXT SESSION DETAILS

NEXT SESSION DATE:	VENUE:
TIME:	DURATION:

NOTES:	

COACHING LOG

DATE:	VENUE:

CLIENT'S NAME:

ADDRESS:

EMAIL:	PHONE NO:
TIME:	DORATION:

TOPIC:

ACTIONS POINTS SINCE THE LAST COACHING SESSION

A.

B.

C.

DISCUSSION SUMMARY

ACTIONS TO WORK ON BEFORE NEXT SESSION

A.

B.

C.

LIGHT BULB MOMENTS

A.

B.

C.

NEXT SESSION DETAILS

NEXT SESSION DATE:	VENUE:
TIME:	DURATION:

NOTES:

COACHING LOG

DATE:	VENUE:

CLIENT'S NAME:	

ADDRESS:	

EMAIL:	PHONE NO:
TIME:	DORATION:

TOPIC:	

ACTIONS POINTS SINCE THE LAST COACHING SESSION

A.	
B.	
C.	

DISCUSSION SUMMARY

ACTIONS TO WORK ON BEFORE NEXT SESSION

A.	
B.	
C.	

LIGHT BULB MOMENTS

A.	
B.	
C.	

NEXT SESSION DETAILS

NEXT SESSION DATE:	VENUE:
TIME:	DURATION:

NOTES:	

COACHING LOG

DATE:	VENUE:

CLIENT'S NAME:

ADDRESS:

EMAIL:	PHONE NO:
TIME:	DORATION:

TOPIC:

ACTIONS POINTS SINCE THE LAST COACHING SESSION

A.

B.

C.

DISCUSSION SUMMARY

ACTIONS TO WORK ON BEFORE NEXT SESSION

A.

B.

C.

LIGHT BULB MOMENTS

A.

B.

C.

NEXT SESSION DETAILS

NEXT SESSION DATE:	VENUE:
TIME:	DURATION:

NOTES:

COACHING LOG

DATE:	VENUE:

CLIENT'S NAME:

ADDRESS:

EMAIL:	PHONE NO:
TIME:	DORATION:

TOPIC:

ACTIONS POINTS SINCE THE LAST COACHING SESSION

A.	
B.	
C.	

DISCUSSION SUMMARY

ACTIONS TO WORK ON BEFORE NEXT SESSION

A.	
B.	
C.	

LIGHT BULB MOMENTS

A.	
B.	
C.	

NEXT SESSION DETAILS

NEXT SESSION DATE:	VENUE:
TIME:	DURATION:

NOTES:

COACHING LOG

DATE:	VENUE:

CLIENT'S NAME:

ADDRESS:

EMAIL:	PHONE NO:
TIME:	DORATION:

TOPIC:

ACTIONS POINTS SINCE THE LAST COACHING SESSION

A.	
B.	
C.	

DISCUSSION SUMMARY

ACTIONS TO WORK ON BEFORE NEXT SESSION

A.	
B.	
C.	

LIGHT BULB MOMENTS

A.	
B.	
C.	

NEXT SESSION DETAILS

NEXT SESSION DATE:	VENUE:
TIME:	DURATION:

NOTES:

COACHING LOG

DATE:	VENUE:

CLIENT'S NAME:	

ADDRESS:

EMAIL:	PHONE NO:
TIME:	DORATION:

TOPIC:

ACTIONS POINTS SINCE THE LAST COACHING SESSION

A.

B.

C.

DISCUSSION SUMMARY

ACTIONS TO WORK ON BEFORE NEXT SESSION

A.

B.

C.

LIGHT BULB MOMENTS

A.

B.

C.

NEXT SESSION DETAILS

NEXT SESSION DATE:	VENUE:
TIME:	DURATION:

NOTES:

COACHING LOG

DATE:	VENUE:

CLIENT'S NAME:

ADDRESS:

EMAIL:	PHONE NO:
TIME:	DORATION:

TOPIC:

ACTIONS POINTS SINCE THE LAST COACHING SESSION

A.	
B.	
C.	

DISCUSSION SUMMARY

ACTIONS TO WORK ON BEFORE NEXT SESSION

A.	
B.	
C.	

LIGHT BULB MOMENTS

A.	
B.	
C.	

NEXT SESSION DETAILS

NEXT SESSION DATE:	VENUE:
TIME:	DURATION:

NOTES:

COACHING LOG

DATE:	VENUE:

CLIENT'S NAME:

ADDRESS:

EMAIL:	PHONE NO:
TIME:	DORATION:

TOPIC:

ACTIONS POINTS SINCE THE LAST COACHING SESSION

A.	
B.	
C.	

DISCUSSION SUMMARY

ACTIONS TO WORK ON BEFORE NEXT SESSION

A.	
B.	
C.	

LIGHT BULB MOMENTS

A.	
B.	
C.	

NEXT SESSION DETAILS

NEXT SESSION DATE:	VENUE:
TIME:	DURATION:

NOTES:

COACHING LOG

DATE:	VENUE:

CLIENT'S NAME:

ADDRESS:

EMAIL:	PHONE NO:
TIME:	DORATION:

TOPIC:

ACTIONS POINTS SINCE THE LAST COACHING SESSION

A.

B.

C.

DISCUSSION SUMMARY

ACTIONS TO WORK ON BEFORE NEXT SESSION

A.

B.

C.

LIGHT BULB MOMENTS

A.

B.

C.

NEXT SESSION DETAILS

NEXT SESSION DATE:	VENUE:
TIME:	DURATION:

NOTES:

COACHING LOG

DATE:	VENUE:

CLIENT'S NAME:

ADDRESS:

EMAIL:	PHONE NO:

TIME:	DORATION:

TOPIC:

ACTIONS POINTS SINCE THE LAST COACHING SESSION

A.	
B.	
C.	

DISCUSSION SUMMARY

ACTIONS TO WORK ON BEFORE NEXT SESSION

A.	
B.	
C.	

LIGHT BULB MOMENTS

A.	
B.	
C.	

NEXT SESSION DETAILS

NEXT SESSION DATE:	VENUE:
TIME:	DURATION:

NOTES:

COACHING LOG

DATE:	VENUE:

CLIENT'S NAME:

ADDRESS:

EMAIL:	PHONE NO:
TIME:	DORATION:

TOPIC:

ACTIONS POINTS SINCE THE LAST COACHING SESSION

A.	
B.	
C.	

DISCUSSION SUMMARY

ACTIONS TO WORK ON BEFORE NEXT SESSION

A.	
B.	
C.	

LIGHT BULB MOMENTS

A.	
B.	
C.	

NEXT SESSION DETAILS

NEXT SESSION DATE:	VENUE:
TIME:	DURATION:

NOTES:

COACHING LOG

DATE:	VENUE:

CLIENT'S NAME:

ADDRESS:

EMAIL:	PHONE NO:
TIME:	DORATION:

TOPIC:

ACTIONS POINTS SINCE THE LAST COACHING SESSION

A.

B.

C.

DISCUSSION SUMMARY

ACTIONS TO WORK ON BEFORE NEXT SESSION

A.

B.

C.

LIGHT BULB MOMENTS

A.

B.

C.

NEXT SESSION DETAILS

NEXT SESSION DATE:	VENUE:
TIME:	DURATION:

NOTES:

COACHING LOG

DATE:	VENUE:

CLIENT'S NAME:

ADDRESS:

EMAIL:	PHONE NO:
TIME:	DORATION:

TOPIC:

ACTIONS POINTS SINCE THE LAST COACHING SESSION

A.	
B.	
C.	

DISCUSSION SUMMARY

ACTIONS TO WORK ON BEFORE NEXT SESSION

A.	
B.	
C.	

LIGHT BULB MOMENTS

A.	
B.	
C.	

NEXT SESSION DETAILS

NEXT SESSION DATE:	VENUE:
TIME:	DURATION:

NOTES:

COACHING LOG

DATE:	VENUE:

CLIENT'S NAME:	

ADDRESS:	

EMAIL:	PHONE NO:
TIME:	DORATION:

TOPIC:	

ACTIONS POINTS SINCE THE LAST COACHING SESSION

A.	
B.	
C.	

DISCUSSION SUMMARY

ACTIONS TO WORK ON BEFORE NEXT SESSION

A.	
B.	
C.	

LIGHT BULB MOMENTS

A.	
B.	
C.	

NEXT SESSION DETAILS

NEXT SESSION DATE:	VENUE:
TIME:	DURATION:

NOTES:	

COACHING LOG

DATE:	VENUE:

CLIENT'S NAME:

ADDRESS:

EMAIL:	PHONE NO:
TIME:	DORATION:

TOPIC:

ACTIONS POINTS SINCE THE LAST COACHING SESSION

A.	
B.	
C.	

DISCUSSION SUMMARY

ACTIONS TO WORK ON BEFORE NEXT SESSION

A.	
B.	
C.	

LIGHT BULB MOMENTS

A.	
B.	
C.	

NEXT SESSION DETAILS

NEXT SESSION DATE:	VENUE:
TIME:	DURATION:

NOTES:

COACHING LOG

DATE:	VENUE:

CLIENT'S NAME:

ADDRESS:

EMAIL:	PHONE NO:
TIME:	DORATION:

TOPIC:

ACTIONS POINTS SINCE THE LAST COACHING SESSION

A.	
B.	
C.	

DISCUSSION SUMMARY

ACTIONS TO WORK ON BEFORE NEXT SESSION

A.	
B.	
C.	

LIGHT BULB MOMENTS

A.	
B.	
C.	

NEXT SESSION DETAILS

NEXT SESSION DATE:	VENUE:
TIME:	DURATION:

NOTES:

COACHING LOG

DATE: | VENUE:

CLIENT'S NAME:

ADDRESS:

EMAIL: | PHONE NO:

TIME: | DORATION:

TOPIC:

ACTIONS POINTS SINCE THE LAST COACHING SESSION

A.

B.

C.

DISCUSSION SUMMARY

ACTIONS TO WORK ON BEFORE NEXT SESSION

A.

B.

C.

LIGHT BULB MOMENTS

A.

B.

C.

NEXT SESSION DETAILS

NEXT SESSION DATE: | VENUE:

TIME: | DURATION:

NOTES:

COACHING LOG

DATE:	VENUE:

CLIENT'S NAME:

ADDRESS:

EMAIL:	PHONE NO:
TIME:	DORATION:

TOPIC:

ACTIONS POINTS SINCE THE LAST COACHING SESSION

A.	
B.	
C.	

DISCUSSION SUMMARY

ACTIONS TO WORK ON BEFORE NEXT SESSION

A.	
B.	
C.	

LIGHT BULB MOMENTS

A.	
B.	
C.	

NEXT SESSION DETAILS

NEXT SESSION DATE:	VENUE:
TIME:	DURATION:

NOTES:

COACHING LOG

DATE:	VENUE:

CLIENT'S NAME:

ADDRESS:

EMAIL:	PHONE NO:
TIME:	DORATION:

TOPIC:

ACTIONS POINTS SINCE THE LAST COACHING SESSION

A.	
B.	
C.	

DISCUSSION SUMMARY

ACTIONS TO WORK ON BEFORE NEXT SESSION

A.	
B.	
C.	

LIGHT BULB MOMENTS

A.	
B.	
C.	

NEXT SESSION DETAILS

NEXT SESSION DATE:	VENUE:
TIME:	DURATION:

NOTES:

COACHING LOG

DATE:	VENUE:

CLIENT'S NAME:

ADDRESS:

EMAIL:	PHONE NO:
TIME:	DORATION:

TOPIC:

ACTIONS POINTS SINCE THE LAST COACHING SESSION

A.

B.

C.

DISCUSSION SUMMARY

ACTIONS TO WORK ON BEFORE NEXT SESSION

A.

B.

C.

LIGHT BULB MOMENTS

A.

B.

C.

NEXT SESSION DETAILS

NEXT SESSION DATE:	VENUE:
TIME:	DURATION:

NOTES:

COACHING LOG

DATE:	VENUE:

CLIENT'S NAME:	

ADDRESS:	

EMAIL:	PHONE NO:

TIME:	DORATION:

TOPIC:	

ACTIONS POINTS SINCE THE LAST COACHING SESSION

A.	
B.	
C.	

DISCUSSION SUMMARY

ACTIONS TO WORK ON BEFORE NEXT SESSION

A.	
B.	
C.	

LIGHT BULB MOMENTS

A.	
B.	
C.	

NEXT SESSION DETAILS

NEXT SESSION DATE:	VENUE:

TIME:	DURATION:

NOTES:	

COACHING LOG

DATE:	VENUE:

CLIENT'S NAME:

ADDRESS:

EMAIL:	PHONE NO:

TIME:	DORATION:

TOPIC:

ACTIONS POINTS SINCE THE LAST COACHING SESSION

A.	
B.	
C.	

DISCUSSION SUMMARY

ACTIONS TO WORK ON BEFORE NEXT SESSION

A.	
B.	
C.	

LIGHT BULB MOMENTS

A.	
B.	
C.	

NEXT SESSION DETAILS

NEXT SESSION DATE:	VENUE:
TIME:	DURATION:

NOTES:

COACHING LOG

DATE:	VENUE:

CLIENT'S NAME:

ADDRESS:

EMAIL:	PHONE NO:
TIME:	DORATION:

TOPIC:

ACTIONS POINTS SINCE THE LAST COACHING SESSION

A.	
B.	
C.	

DISCUSSION SUMMARY

ACTIONS TO WORK ON BEFORE NEXT SESSION

A.	
B.	
C.	

LIGHT BULB MOMENTS

A.	
B.	
C.	

NEXT SESSION DETAILS

NEXT SESSION DATE:	VENUE:
TIME:	DURATION:

NOTES:

COACHING LOG

DATE:	VENUE:

CLIENT'S NAME:

ADDRESS:

EMAIL:	PHONE NO:

TIME:	DORATION:

TOPIC:

ACTIONS POINTS SINCE THE LAST COACHING SESSION

A.	
B.	
C.	

DISCUSSION SUMMARY

ACTIONS TO WORK ON BEFORE NEXT SESSION

A.	
B.	
C.	

LIGHT BULB MOMENTS

A.	
B.	
C.	

NEXT SESSION DETAILS

NEXT SESSION DATE:	VENUE:
TIME:	DURATION:

NOTES:

COACHING LOG

DATE:	VENUE:

CLIENT'S NAME:

ADDRESS:

EMAIL:	PHONE NO:
TIME:	DORATION:

TOPIC:

ACTIONS POINTS SINCE THE LAST COACHING SESSION

A.

B.

C.

DISCUSSION SUMMARY

ACTIONS TO WORK ON BEFORE NEXT SESSION

A.

B.

C.

LIGHT BULB MOMENTS

A.

B.

C.

NEXT SESSION DETAILS

NEXT SESSION DATE:	VENUE:
TIME:	DURATION:

NOTES:

COACHING LOG

DATE:	VENUE:

CLIENT'S NAME:

ADDRESS:

EMAIL:	PHONE NO:
TIME:	DORATION:

TOPIC:

ACTIONS POINTS SINCE THE LAST COACHING SESSION

A.

B.

C.

DISCUSSION SUMMARY

ACTIONS TO WORK ON BEFORE NEXT SESSION

A.

B.

C.

LIGHT BULB MOMENTS

A.

B.

C.

NEXT SESSION DETAILS

NEXT SESSION DATE:	VENUE:
TIME:	DURATION:

NOTES:

COACHING LOG

DATE:	VENUE:

CLIENT'S NAME:

ADDRESS:

EMAIL:	PHONE NO:
TIME:	DORATION:

TOPIC:

ACTIONS POINTS SINCE THE LAST COACHING SESSION

A.	
B.	
C.	

DISCUSSION SUMMARY

ACTIONS TO WORK ON BEFORE NEXT SESSION

A.	
B.	
C.	

LIGHT BULB MOMENTS

A.	
B.	
C.	

NEXT SESSION DETAILS

NEXT SESSION DATE:	VENUE:
TIME:	DURATION:

NOTES:

COACHING LOG

DATE:	VENUE:

CLIENT'S NAME:	

ADDRESS:	

EMAIL:	PHONE NO:
TIME:	DORATION:

TOPIC:	

ACTIONS POINTS SINCE THE LAST COACHING SESSION

A.	
B.	
C.	

DISCUSSION SUMMARY

ACTIONS TO WORK ON BEFORE NEXT SESSION

A.	
B.	
C.	

LIGHT BULB MOMENTS

A.	
B.	
C.	

NEXT SESSION DETAILS

NEXT SESSION DATE:	VENUE:
TIME:	DURATION:

NOTES:	

COACHING LOG

DATE:	VENUE:

CLIENT'S NAME:

ADDRESS:

EMAIL:	PHONE NO:
TIME:	DORATION:

TOPIC:

ACTIONS POINTS SINCE THE LAST COACHING SESSION

A.	
B.	
C.	

DISCUSSION SUMMARY

ACTIONS TO WORK ON BEFORE NEXT SESSION

A.	
B.	
C.	

LIGHT BULB MOMENTS

A.	
B.	
C.	

NEXT SESSION DETAILS

NEXT SESSION DATE:	VENUE:
TIME:	DURATION:

NOTES:

COACHING LOG

DATE:	VENUE:

CLIENT'S NAME:

ADDRESS:

EMAIL:	PHONE NO:

TIME:	DORATION:

TOPIC:

ACTIONS POINTS SINCE THE LAST COACHING SESSION

A.	
B.	
C.	

DISCUSSION SUMMARY

ACTIONS TO WORK ON BEFORE NEXT SESSION

A.	
B.	
C.	

LIGHT BULB MOMENTS

A.	
B.	
C.	

NEXT SESSION DETAILS

NEXT SESSION DATE:	VENUE:
TIME:	DURATION:

NOTES:

COACHING LOG

DATE:	VENUE:

CLIENT'S NAME:

ADDRESS:

EMAIL:	PHONE NO:
TIME:	DORATION:

TOPIC:

ACTIONS POINTS SINCE THE LAST COACHING SESSION

A.	
B.	
C.	

DISCUSSION SUMMARY

ACTIONS TO WORK ON BEFORE NEXT SESSION

A.	
B.	
C.	

LIGHT BULB MOMENTS

A.	
B.	
C.	

NEXT SESSION DETAILS

NEXT SESSION DATE:	VENUE:
TIME:	DURATION:

NOTES:

COACHING LOG

DATE:	VENUE:

CLIENT'S NAME:	

ADDRESS:

EMAIL:	PHONE NO:
TIME:	DORATION:

TOPIC:

ACTIONS POINTS SINCE THE LAST COACHING SESSION

A.

B.

C.

DISCUSSION SUMMARY

ACTIONS TO WORK ON BEFORE NEXT SESSION

A.

B.

C.

LIGHT BULB MOMENTS

A.

B.

C.

NEXT SESSION DETAILS

NEXT SESSION DATE:	VENUE:
TIME:	DURATION:

NOTES:

COACHING LOG

DATE:	VENUE:

CLIENT'S NAME:

ADDRESS:

EMAIL:	PHONE NO:
TIME:	DORATION:

TOPIC:

ACTIONS POINTS SINCE THE LAST COACHING SESSION

A.	
B.	
C.	

DISCUSSION SUMMARY

ACTIONS TO WORK ON BEFORE NEXT SESSION

A.	
B.	
C.	

LIGHT BULB MOMENTS

A.	
B.	
C.	

NEXT SESSION DETAILS

NEXT SESSION DATE:	VENUE:
TIME:	DURATION:

NOTES:

COACHING LOG

DATE:	VENUE:

CLIENT'S NAME:

ADDRESS:

EMAIL:	PHONE NO:
TIME:	DORATION:

TOPIC:

ACTIONS POINTS SINCE THE LAST COACHING SESSION

A.	
B.	
C.	

DISCUSSION SUMMARY

ACTIONS TO WORK ON BEFORE NEXT SESSION

A.	
B.	
C.	

LIGHT BULB MOMENTS

A.	
B.	
C.	

NEXT SESSION DETAILS

NEXT SESSION DATE:	VENUE:
TIME:	DURATION:

NOTES:

COACHING LOG

DATE:	VENUE:

CLIENT'S NAME:

ADDRESS:

EMAIL:	PHONE NO:
TIME:	DORATION:

TOPIC:

ACTIONS POINTS SINCE THE LAST COACHING SESSION

A.	
B.	
C.	

DISCUSSION SUMMARY

ACTIONS TO WORK ON BEFORE NEXT SESSION

A.	
B.	
C.	

LIGHT BULB MOMENTS

A.	
B.	
C.	

NEXT SESSION DETAILS

NEXT SESSION DATE:	VENUE:
TIME:	DURATION:

NOTES:

COACHING LOG

DATE:	VENUE:

CLIENT'S NAME:

ADDRESS:

EMAIL:	PHONE NO:
TIME:	DORATION:

TOPIC:

ACTIONS POINTS SINCE THE LAST COACHING SESSION

A.
B.
C.

DISCUSSION SUMMARY

ACTIONS TO WORK ON BEFORE NEXT SESSION

A.
B.
C.

LIGHT BULB MOMENTS

A.
B.
C.

NEXT SESSION DETAILS

NEXT SESSION DATE:	VENUE:
TIME:	DURATION:

NOTES:

COACHING LOG

DATE:	VENUE:

CLIENT'S NAME:

ADDRESS:

EMAIL:	PHONE NO:
TIME:	DORATION:

TOPIC:

ACTIONS POINTS SINCE THE LAST COACHING SESSION

A.	
B.	
C.	

DISCUSSION SUMMARY

ACTIONS TO WORK ON BEFORE NEXT SESSION

A.	
B.	
C.	

LIGHT BULB MOMENTS

A.	
B.	
C.	

NEXT SESSION DETAILS

NEXT SESSION DATE:	VENUE:
TIME:	DURATION:

NOTES:

COACHING LOG

DATE:	VENUE:

CLIENT'S NAME:	

ADDRESS:	

EMAIL:	PHONE NO:
TIME:	DORATION:

TOPIC:	

ACTIONS POINTS SINCE THE LAST COACHING SESSION

A.	
B.	
C.	

DISCUSSION SUMMARY

ACTIONS TO WORK ON BEFORE NEXT SESSION

A.	
B.	
C.	

LIGHT BULB MOMENTS

A.	
B.	
C.	

NEXT SESSION DETAILS

NEXT SESSION DATE:	VENUE:
TIME:	DURATION:

NOTES:	

COACHING LOG

DATE:	VENUE:

CLIENT'S NAME:

ADDRESS:

EMAIL:	PHONE NO:
TIME:	DORATION:

TOPIC:

ACTIONS POINTS SINCE THE LAST COACHING SESSION

A.	
B.	
C.	

DISCUSSION SUMMARY

ACTIONS TO WORK ON BEFORE NEXT SESSION

A.	
B.	
C.	

LIGHT BULB MOMENTS

A.	
B.	
C.	

NEXT SESSION DETAILS

NEXT SESSION DATE:	VENUE:
TIME:	DURATION:

NOTES:

COACHING LOG

DATE:	VENUE:

CLIENT'S NAME:

ADDRESS:

EMAIL:	PHONE NO:

TIME:	DORATION:

TOPIC:

ACTIONS POINTS SINCE THE LAST COACHING SESSION

A.	
B.	
C.	

DISCUSSION SUMMARY

ACTIONS TO WORK ON BEFORE NEXT SESSION

A.	
B.	
C.	

LIGHT BULB MOMENTS

A.	
B.	
C.	

NEXT SESSION DETAILS

NEXT SESSION DATE:	VENUE:
TIME:	DURATION:

NOTES:

COACHING LOG

DATE:	VENUE:

CLIENT'S NAME:

ADDRESS:

EMAIL:	PHONE NO:
TIME:	DORATION:

TOPIC:

ACTIONS POINTS SINCE THE LAST COACHING SESSION

A.

B.

C.

DISCUSSION SUMMARY

ACTIONS TO WORK ON BEFORE NEXT SESSION

A.

B.

C.

LIGHT BULB MOMENTS

A.

B.

C.

NEXT SESSION DETAILS

NEXT SESSION DATE:	VENUE:
TIME:	DURATION:

NOTES:

COACHING LOG

DATE:	VENUE:

CLIENT'S NAME:	

ADDRESS:	

EMAIL:	PHONE NO:
TIME:	DORATION:

TOPIC:	

ACTIONS POINTS SINCE THE LAST COACHING SESSION

A.	
B.	
C.	

DISCUSSION SUMMARY

ACTIONS TO WORK ON BEFORE NEXT SESSION

A.	
B.	
C.	

LIGHT BULB MOMENTS

A.	
B.	
C.	

NEXT SESSION DETAILS

NEXT SESSION DATE:	VENUE:
TIME:	DURATION:

NOTES:	

COACHING LOG

DATE:	VENUE:

CLIENT'S NAME:

ADDRESS:

EMAIL:	PHONE NO:
TIME:	DORATION:

TOPIC:

ACTIONS POINTS SINCE THE LAST COACHING SESSION

A.	
B.	
C.	

DISCUSSION SUMMARY

ACTIONS TO WORK ON BEFORE NEXT SESSION

A.	
B.	
C.	

LIGHT BULB MOMENTS

A.	
B.	
C.	

NEXT SESSION DETAILS

NEXT SESSION DATE:	VENUE:
TIME:	DURATION:

NOTES:

COACHING LOG

DATE:	VENUE:

CLIENT'S NAME:

ADDRESS:

EMAIL:	PHONE NO:
TIME:	DORATION:

TOPIC:

ACTIONS POINTS SINCE THE LAST COACHING SESSION

A.	
B.	
C.	

DISCUSSION SUMMARY

ACTIONS TO WORK ON BEFORE NEXT SESSION

A.	
B.	
C.	

LIGHT BULB MOMENTS

A.	
B.	
C.	

NEXT SESSION DETAILS

NEXT SESSION DATE:	VENUE:
TIME:	DURATION:

NOTES:

Thank You For Shopping With us

Printed in Great Britain
by Amazon